A LIFE THAT MEASURES WITH THE LIFE OF GOD

by

Camron Schofield

Published by

Eternal Realities

Copyright © 2015

ISBN: 978-0-9941997-8-2

www.eternalrealities.com

Contents

CHAPTER 1 5
Salvation depends upon our sense of need [5] Blind to our true condition [5] No sense of need without recognition of our true condition [5] We are living in uncertain times [6] How shall we be awakened to our sense of need? [6] Confused Christian experiences [7] The law has been perverted [7] My experience [8] Because the law has been perverted, life's experiences must now lead us to Christ – yet we may still miss the lesson [9]

CHAPTER 2 10
Of ourselves we cannot do anything right [10] Don't be envious of those who appear to have a fortunate life [10] Admitting that we cannot do it right and letting God do it [11] We must be petrified of living our own life [12] The gift of a new life [12] God came to us as a human being [13] He gave up everything for us [13] Christ had no advantage over us – He could do nothing of Himself [14]

CHAPTER 3 16
Our only power is choice [16] Christ could do nothing of Himself [16] The Father did the works [17] God's works are perfect [17] Christ was the visible expression of the Father [18] The life of God [18] What the Father produced in the life of Christ He was producing in us [18] It is not I that live but Christ that lives in me [19] The life of God without being God [20]

CHAPTER 4 21
Christ was born of the Spirit [21] How the Father lived in Christ [22] The power of God is in His word [22] The word worked within Christ [23] Ten promises [24]

CHAPTER 5 26
The power of God unto salvation [26] Christ read the word of God as speaking to Himself [26] He took the promises personally [27] The faith of Jesus [28]

CHAPTER 6 30
The same privilege is offered to us [30] Christ is our example [30] A broken spirit and a contrite heart is God's own sacrifice [31] That

which issues out of the heart of God [31] The flesh and blood of Christ [32] The word is the life [33]

CHAPTER 7 34
Reading ourselves into the word [34] Never try to hide your sins from God [35] Christ took the blame for all our sins and confessed them even though He never committed them [36] We also must confess all [36] The "Acceptable Time" [37] I die daily [38]

CHAPTER 8 39
Christ became one with every individual [39] Except Christ became ourselves He could not save us [39] When He died we died [40] Christ was one with me [40] The Holy Spirit will show us our future life [41] Christ rested in His Father's love during the storm and so can we [42] To "believe" is to receive the life of Christ as my own [42]

CHAPTER 9 44
Abraham's belief [44] The promised child could not be born until Abraham's faith received God's word [44] Christ came to Abraham as himself [46] Christ met Joshua as himself [46] Christ shared the experience with Shadrach, Meshach, and Abednego [47] Jacob meets his equal [47] Their Saviour is our Saviour [49]

CHAPTER 10 50
What it means to "know" Christ [50] Receiving the heart of Christ [50] The Apostle Peter [50] John the Beloved [51] The Apostle Paul [53] Martin Luther [54] John Bunyan [55] Charles Spurgeon [55] The desperate [55] The charge of blasphemy against Christ will be hurled at His followers today [56] We do not become God [56] A life that measures with the life of God [57] A prayer [57]

CHAPTER 1

Salvation depends upon our sense of need

Our salvation depends entirely upon our sense of need. Some may argue that our salvation depends entirely upon Christ. Indeed. But our reliance upon Christ will be in proportion to our sense of need. Christ came to be a healer for the sin-sick. But those that are not sick have no need of a physician (Matthew 9:12). With these words, Christ implied that there are those who will never benefit from the gift of His salvation because they do not seek His help. A doctor cannot help us unless we go to his surgery, or we call him to our home. Likewise, except we come to Christ or call after Him, there is no healing from sin.

Blind to our true condition

The True Witness of Revelation chapter 3 describes the condition of those who are unwilling to acknowledge their condition as "Laodicean". They say, "I am rich, and increased with goods, and have need of nothing"; but know not that in reality they are "wretched, and miserable, and poor, and blind, and naked" (Revelation 3:14-17). In another sense, when speaking to Israel through Isaiah, God described the true condition of their whole head and their whole heart as sick and faint. "From the sole of the foot even unto the head there is no soundness... but wounds, and bruises, and putrifying sores" (Isaiah 1:5-6). Yet they boasted in their supposed purity and separated themselves from those who they termed "other men" (Luke 18:11), crying, "Come not near to me; for I am holier than thou" (Isaiah 65:5).

No sense of need without recognition of our true condition

The apostle Paul testified of his own experience with the truthfulness of these two testimonies. He declared that he was an Hebrew of the Hebrews, of the tribe of Benjamin, as touching the law, blameless (Philippians 3:5-6). Yet when He met Christ on the road to Damascus, the blackness of his soul was revealed and he cried out, "Who shall save me from the body of this death!" For when the law came, sin revived and he died. He saw that what he wanted to do, he could not do and vice versa. When he discovered who he really was without Christ, he became conscious of his inherently wicked nature. (Romans 7.)

For a long time, Paul was oblivious to his true condition. But when he saw the glory of God, he saw himself as he really was. Isaiah's experience was the same. When the sins of Israel were exposed, he stood aloof, considering himself as not included in the denunciation, but when he saw God, he confessed, "Woe is me! for I am undone; because I am a man of unclean lips, and I dwell in the midst of a people of unclean lips" (Isaiah 6:5).

We are living in uncertain times

To be without Christ is a terrible thing. This is a very uncertain world. From social commotions to natural upheavals, we know not what tomorrow may bring and "sufficient unto the day is the evil thereof." (Matthew 6:34). It is all too true that this very day, or even moment, may be our last. Have we made peace with God? Is our conscience clear? We should be asking ourselves these questions far more than we do for we know not when the "silver cord [shall] be loosed" (Ecclesiastes 12:6).

How shall we be awakened to our sense of need?

How then shall we be awakened to our sense of need? This is a fair question. The scriptures declare that the goodness of God leads us to repentance (Romans 2:4). When we contemplate that God did not abandon us despite how rebellious we were, our hearts are touched; whether it be in the context of man's first rebellion in the Garden of Eden, or our very own past lives. "When we were enemies we were reconciled to God by the death of His Son" (Romans 5:10). It was "while we were yet sinners, [that] Christ died for us" (Romans 5:8). "He (God) first loved us" (1 John 4:19). We did not search for God, but God came in search of us – *despite* our wretchedness. Even though "my wounds stink and are corrupt because of my foolishness. . ." and "my lovers and my friends stand aloof from my sore" (Psalm 38:5, 11), He is not repulsed by the stench of sin, but even lays His own pure cloak upon us to cover our nakedness (Luke 15:20-23). He "punishe[s] us less than our iniquities deserve (Ezra 9:13) and then "cast[s] all [our] sins into the depths of the sea," saying, "I will remember their sin no more" (Micah 7:19, Jeremiah 31:34).

Confused Christian experiences

But all this, while as beautiful and touching as it is, may fail of waking us up to our condition. I have seen many a "Christian" rejoice in this and yet have no sense of need. They take the love of God for granted and make merchandise of it (2 Corinthians 2:17, *Geneva Bible*). There are those, perhaps, who have been brought up in a church and have been taught by their parents and teachers that they are sinners. How many shake this thought off as they get older, casting the conviction aside as a burden to their worldly aspirations? It is true, however, that a few will retain these things in their thoughts and will bow in humility before God. But of them, how many serve Him out of fear, rather than out of love?

The goodness of God will lead you to repentance. But who will lead you to Christ that He may "give repentance" to you? (Acts 5:31, 2 Timothy 2:25.)

Those that know God through nature do not necessarily know a God of love. They may see only a God of power and judgment. Or a God of order. Few will see Him as a God of love in the delicately tinted flowers with their delightful fragrances and of pure selflessness in the ocean that takes to give.

The law has been perverted

There was a time when the law of God was the "schoolmaster to bring us unto Christ" (Galatians 3:24). Yes. That time still is. "For by the law is the knowledge of sin" (Romans 3:20). And except we see that we are sinners, we will not come to Christ. But "the law, the law, the law" has been very indelicately forced into people's lives so that the aversion to it is far greater than ever in earth's history. The law has been abused and misrepresented and God will not hold the world accountable for their treatment of His law if it has been incorrectly represented to them by those who profess to be the "repositories of His law". Those who are expecting the heavens to declare His righteousness by the showing of the tables of stone (Psalm 50:6, 97:6) this side of mankind's probation, will be disappointed. It will not be the law that will condemn sinners in this age, but it is the *gospel* that shall be preached to all nations for a witness (Matthew 24:14).

It is sad that the law has been so falsely represented and therefore so universally maligned. But this especially is where the words of Jesus apply: "They know not what they do." (Luke 23:34) Because of the misconceptions that many have of the law, I shall endeavour to speak of it as little as possible. Like Paul, I will seek to be "to them that are without law, as without law. . . that I might gain them that are without law" (1 Corinthians 9:21).

Yet that would be the most perfect verse to answer our query: How then shall we be awakened to our sense of need? If we are "without law?" The simple answer is: life's experiences.

My experience

Permit me to explain by a brief account of my own experience in no more than five sentences. I was told from a very early age that I was a sinner and that I could be sure my sins will find me out (Numbers 32:23). I tried hard to be good, but lived under a heavy burden of guilt. I was told that Jesus would forgive my sins; and so I confessed them to Him and found momentary respite before failing once more. The more I looked at the law and tried to keep it, the more impossible it became, resulting in a constant cloud of self-condemnation (yet thinking that it was God's condemnation). It wasn't until my outwardly righteous life began to fall apart that I began to seek Christ with genuine earnestness.

Some may compare my experience to that of Esau who came weeping and repenting because of the consequences (Hebrews 12:17). But we are not here talking about repentance. We are talking about coming to Christ. We must come to Christ before He can give us repentance. The peace of forgiveness is one thing, but a life of peace is something else. Forgiveness is the band-aid, but it is not the cure. Salvation in Christ is more than just forgiveness of sins. "If we confess our sins he is faithful and just to forgive us our sins *and* to cleanse us from all unrighteousness" (1 John 1:9).

Because the law has been perverted, life's experiences must now lead us to Christ – yet we may still miss the lesson

Life's experiences are what will awaken us to our sense of need – nothing short of it. Few will be woken in any other way. The problem with Laodicea is that her life was too easy. She had need of nothing – she already had everything (she thought). She was at ease and like Sodom, everything came without effort (Genesis 13:10). It is when the storm rages that the sailors cry to God for help (Psalm 107:23-30).

What, though, when the storm ceases and they return safe to the port? Do they thank God for their deliverance and continue in His ways? Or do they return to the bar, drinking and revelling? We are all sailors on the sea of life. We cry to God for help when the going gets tough and the waves threaten to drown us. But when the sea is calm again, we forget our deliverer and we sail wherever our whims and notions will blow us.

We may yet miss the lesson life's experiences should teach us. If we would have Christ continually with us, we must be continually needing Him. This constant realization of our need can only be our experience when we recognize our *condition*.

CHAPTER 2

Of ourselves we cannot do anything right

Isaiah says that all our right-doings are as filthy rags and our iniquities blow us away like the wind blows away a leaf (Isaiah 64:6). Consider that thought. Righteousness is right-doing – right works/acts etc... Is Isaiah saying that it doesn't matter how "right" we may do something, it is still wrong? Consider also the words of the wise man that we are to guard the heart because out of it are the issues of life (Proverbs 4:23). That word "issues" means what comes out of it, like products on a production line – that which the heart produces. Combine that thought with the following verse that says "the heart is deceitful above all things and desperately wicked: who can know it?" (Jeremiah 17:9). The heart is deceitful and wicked; therefore what will come out of it is deception and wickedness. No? Surely not my heart! Surely so. The heart is so deceitful that the Scriptures had to repeat five times that there is "none that doeth good"... etc.! (Psalm 14:1, 3, 53:1, 3, Romans 3:12); and still we forget it. Let me sum this up another way:

You cannot do anything right.

Don't be envious of those who appear to have a fortunate life

Now, before you close this book and throw it away, please give me a moment. For some people, like me, whatever they touch falls apart. For others, everything they touch "turns to gold". They're just really good at what they do. They have what you could call the "Midas touch". Do you know where that phrase comes from? It comes from a story in Greek mythology. King Midas asked the gods to give him the power to make everything he touched turn to gold. Consequently, in a very short time he became a very rich man. But let me tell you the rest of the story. When the evening came and he was hungry, the grapes turned to gold the moment he took the bunch in his hand! He couldn't chew them – or anything else on his table. It all turned to gold the moment he touched it. And it was no different with the wine. Some versions say that at his touch, his own daughter turned to gold! The blessing became a curse and he pleaded for the power to be taken away.

It may appear that you are a very fortunate creature and that those whose lives are nothing but a trail of destruction are less fortunate. But those "poor and afflicted" (Zephaniah 3:12) cry unto God day and night (Luke 18:7) to deliver them from their own selves, while you who carry on in your life, for the time being, think that everything is alright. But in the evening the sweet will be bitter upon your lips, and you will find that which you thought a blessing to be a curse. The heart is deceitful and what you think is so right will one day turn out to be so wrong.

Admitting that we cannot do it right and letting God do it

This is not all doom and gloom and apparently negative psychology. I know it is not an easy thing to admit that we have made a mess of the life that God has given us, but there is nothing lost in doing so. Rather, if we will only acknowledge that we have failed with our trust and then lay our lives at His feet, He will take it and make it right. We may at times wrest them from His hands, and ruin it again, but if we do so, let us believe that nonetheless, He will still be happy to take it back and make it right once more. But if we will learn that every time we take our lives into our own hands we mess it up, then we will fear to lay hold of it and leave it where it is safe – in the hands of Jesus. As they rightly say to those at their wits end, "Let go and let God." And then leave it with Him. Period.

Who is there that wouldn't like a life where God sorts everything out? Such a life would be free from guilt and condemnation; a life where everything is done right and the only consequences are persecution for the sake of that right-doing. Who is there that likes to reap the harvest of their own actions or the bitter fruits of their own planting? Just think: if you will let go and let God, and He is the one who is governing your life, then if anything goes "wrong", it's His problem, right? And He will fix it. It's not for you to worry about. That sounds pretty good to me. In fact, I am afraid to get out of bed in the morning if it is "me" that will be governing my life that day.

And not only will He take care of things in the future, but He will also sort out all the mistakes we have made in the past. He never gets rid of the consequences of our actions, but He will often orchestrate the events, and even the hearts of others, so they are not too heavy that we cannot bear it. But whatever happens, we will never be alone for He will hold our hand through it all.

We must be petrified of living our own life

Sounds good doesn't it? It's even better in experience. Although, I myself am still learning to let go and let God – forever! My sense of need is not yet as great as it ought to be. My heart is very deceitful and before I know it I have taken my life back into my own hands. I am praying that God will fine tune my senses so I know when I have done this, because in my conscious mind, I am petrified of living my own life. But this is why so many people's lives just never seem to work out right – God is constantly having to remind us that we cannot do it. I am saddened by how many people in this world have lost homes, families, jobs, etc. and still won't admit that they have been irresponsible with their lives. So many that live in even the gutters of the streets are too proud to reach out to God to help them. Let's learn now, before something else crashes down around us.

The gift of a new life

The life that God is offering us is a life that surpasses our wildest dreams. It is more than just a life free from guilt and condemnation and having to worry about circumstances. God "is able to do exceeding abundantly above all that we ask or think" (Ephesians 3:20).

God has brought this gift within the reach of every one of us, and He is just waiting for us to accept it. But in bringing to us this gift, He could not come directly to us because we would be like Adam and run and hide ourselves. His glory would overwhelm us. In fact, we would be killed by the brightness of His coming.

The glory of His purity would destroy our sins, and by our attachment to them we would be destroyed also. Therefore He had to bring this gift to us in a different way.

God came to us as a human being

Human beings relate better with those that are in a similar situation and can understand their experience. This is basic social science. And these are laws that God Himself has implanted in humankind. A perfect illustration of this truth is that when Adam was naming all the animals in the Garden of Eden, he saw that there wasn't a mate for him (Genesis 2:19-20); and so God took a rib from his side and made him a companion – one with him in the same nature and who could share life's experiences with him.

Likewise, this is how God needed to approach us. He needed to come to us in the form of a human being. But not just in outward form, but also in the inward realities – the mind and the conscience and their interactions with sinful tendencies. Therefore Christ was made in all things like His brethren (Hebrews 2:17). There was not a thing in which He was not like us. "In all things" does not exclude anything. The one area of difference was that He was "yet without sin" (Hebrews 4:15). This is meant only in the sense that every act in His life was performed right – not as our "right acts" are performed, but according to divine perfection. He was not exempt from the internal struggles that we have. Temptation itself is not sin; it is when we hold onto a wrong thought in the mind that we commit sin. Jesus had to watch and guard the entrance of every thought in the same way that we do.

He gave up everything for us

Was He one with us in our inherent inabilities to produce a life of perfection? He was God, was He not? Indeed He was. However, He had laid everything down that pertains to His Godhead, except the right to its title. Previous to coming to this earth, He was omniscient – that means that He knew everything – past, present, future – all of it. Everything. Even what you are thinking right now. But He left that all behind and became a little babe in a manger and grew in wisdom and in stature just as you and I (Luke 2:40). He was a learner just like you and me, and all that He knew about God He had to learn just like we have to.

Christ was also omnipotent. Yet He gave this up also and when they laid the cross upon His shoulders, He could not bear it. Also, as God, Christ was omnipresent. He could be anywhere at any time at the same time and in any form He so desired. Yet He lost this also when He took upon Himself our humanity. The glory of His divinity with its omnipotence and omniscience returned to Him when He rose from the dead, but He will forever remain in His human form, (though it will be somewhat more spiritual than our earthly state), for there will be those who will ask Him, "What are these wounds in thine hands?" (Zechariah 13:6).

Christ had no advantage over us – He could do nothing of Himself

If He had retained any of these divine qualities when He came to this earth to walk among us, He would have been of no help to us. He could not have identified Himself with us or we with Him. It would all have been a failure. We needed to see someone in our own experience, with absolutely no advantage over us whatsoever. This will become clearer as we proceed.

If Jesus Christ had performed His own works, He would have failed to be our perfect example. He had absolutely no advantage over us whatsoever. He was just as human as you and I. Now, I am not making Jesus out to be a sinner, for human nature itself is not sin. According to James, our nature entices us to sin, yet if the thought is repulsed as hateful, the soul is not corrupted (James 1:13-15). He states that God cannot be tempted with evil. Truly. But Paul writes that Christ was "tempted in all points like as we are" (Hebrews 4:15) (but without sin). Why? Because He was made in the likeness of sinful flesh (Romans 8:3). What does this mean? Simply that He also had a nature that of itself can do nothing right. This is why it was that He "offered up prayers and supplications with strong crying and tears unto Him that was able to save Him from death." (Hebrews 5:7).

You may cry, "Blasphemy!" yet I know my Christ. And you

can know Him too. I pity those who think that Christ had an advantage over them. They are missing out on a wonderful truth. When I was younger, I would take my little trials to my dad and he would say, "Take them to Jesus – He understands." I concluded that He could because He was omniscient; but it never really satisfied me. I needed someone who knew how I was feeling because they had been through the same experience. And as I grew older, I learned that all my trials stemmed from my wicked human heart and I still needed the same kind of friend. But no. Jesus was no different to you and me. He struggled with evil thoughts too – He just didn't cherish them like we do. He was always on guard and repulsed them the instant He discerned their wickedness so that they never took up a moment of His thoughts. Anything short of this, Jesus is no Saviour.

CHAPTER 3

Our only power is choice

The one thing that we need to understand is that there are two influences working upon the minds of men and women – the Scriptures call them the *Spirit* and the *flesh* (Galatians 5:17). As to which mind is operating sovereignty within us is up to us. If we choose to dwell on sinful thoughts (minding the things of the flesh (Romans 8:5)), they will produce themselves in the life. But if we devote the mind to "whatsoever things are pure [and] whatsoever things are lovely" (Philippians 4:8), then we will do the works of the Spirit. The heart is deceitful and desperately wicked, but iniquity doesn't need to issue forth. It can be prevented. Just in the same manner as we obey the wrong, we may obey the right – thoughts and suggestions come to us and we choose which one we want (Joshua 24:15; Romans 6:19). Simple really. Although, not so easy in practice. Not yet, anyway. This spiritual element in mankind is nothing inherent, but ours only through the grace of God placing a supernatural "enmity" within us between the good and the bad (Genesis 3:15). While we do not have the power to *do* the good, He gave us the power to at least *choose* the good.

Christ could do nothing of Himself

Christ's experience was no different to ours. All that He could do was choose to do right. He had to cry with "strong crying and tears" (Hebrews 5:7). Why? Because He came to show us the only way that we can have the victories that we are needing in our lives. He said, "I can of My own self do nothing", "I do nothing of My self " (John 5:30; 8:28). *I do not do My own works*. Is this not self-explanatory? He says He could not. If He had done so, He would have failed to be our perfect example and our salvation would have been lost. Shall we under-estimate the sacrifice God made in placing all of heaven and eternity at risk for our salvation? Imagine how close it came to all falling apart. Consider Christ tempted in the wilderness after forty days of fasting and the devil appears to him saying, "Make these stones as bread" (Matthew 4:3). How easy it is for you to compromise when you are starving and there is nothing else to eat except that which will violate your conscience? No one was looking, surely Christ could have made the rocks bread and eaten them. Right? And Gethsemane – three times His humanity shrank from the sacrifice. How willing are we to bear the blame of others for something that we never did? Christ, who never sinned, submitted to being blamed for the sins of everyone who ever lived. Thank God His love for you was greater than His love for Himself!

The Father did the works

Christ said, "I can of My own self do nothing"; "the Father that dwelleth in Me, He doeth the works" (John 14:10). Here was His salvation. And here it is for us. Having taken upon Himself fallen humanity, Christ could not produce a perfect life by Himself. *But* were He to *permit* God to work *through* Him as a transparent medium, then His life could be filled with perfection. By saying throughout His entire life, "Into thy hands I commend My spirit" (Luke 23:46) the Great Potter was able to mould the life of His precious clay. It was not Christ but the Father who did the works.

God's works are perfect

In Daniel's prayer of confession on behalf of the entire nation of Israel, he prayed, "The Lord our God is righteous in all His works which He doeth" (Daniel 9:14). In other words, all that God does is right. Perfect. Pure. Holy. His heart is pure and therefore all that issues forth from it is as the water of life that flows from His throne. He is the standard of perfection. Anything short of such, is no perfection. He is eternal, and all they that spend eternity with Him must be holy even as He is holy (Matthew 5:48; 1 Peter 1:16). The redeemed will walk with Him in white for they are worthy (Revelation 3:4). Amos asks, "Can two walk together, except they be agreed?" (Amos 3:3).

Christ did not live His own life. The Father lived His life through His Son. When Christ raised the dead to life, it was not by His own power but in the strength of the Father. Christ had no more power to raise the dead to life and calm the stormy sea than you or I do. It was the Father that did it. Christ simply let God work through Him.

Christ was the visible expression of the Father

In another aspect of Christ's life, we see the manifestation of His love toward sinful humanity. He ate and drank with publicans and harlots (Luke 5:30). To the adulterer, He said, "Neither do I condemn thee" (John 8:11), and to the sick of the palsy, "Thy sin be forgiven thee" (Matthew 9:2). But this was not the manifestation of Christ, for He said, "No man knoweth the Son, but the Father"; He came to reveal the Father (Matthew 11:27), and the love that He manifested was the love of the Father toward the sinner. Christ was no "intercessor" shielding man from the wrath of God. He was the visible expression of the Father's heart longing to draw us unto Himself once more.

The life of God

Christ's life was a life that measured with the life of the Father because it was the life of the Father itself. The life of Christ was the life of God. Not because Christ was God, for He had laid His divinity aside, but because Christ became human and as a human He let God live His own life through Him.

In Christ we are all one (Galatians 3:28). As Christ was in the Father, so we are in Him. And through Him, we are in the Father. We are to abide in Christ; for without Him we can do nothing (John 15:4). But He of His own self could no nothing. Yet if we will abide in Him we can bring forth good works. How can this be?

What the Father produced in the life of Christ He was producing in us

Christ was in the "bosom of the Father" (John 1:18) – He was in the Father. And if we are in Him, then we are in the Father even as He is. He is one with us and we are one with Him and if He is one with the Father, then we are one with the Father also. "That they also may be one in Us" (John 17:23). Therefore what the Father produced in the life of Christ, He was producing in our own lives. The life of Christ was our own life. Consider this.

When Christ was raised, we were raised with Him (Hosea 6:2). Right now we sit in heavenly places because He is one with us (Ephesians 1:20, 2:6). Yet He is also in this world "because as He is, so are we in this world" (1 John 4:17). He is so perfectly identified with us that where He is we are there also. This is not only true in the future time He refers to in His promise, "I will come again, and receive you unto myself; that where I am, there ye may be also." (John 14:3) but we are with Him now for He says, "I am with you always, even unto the end of the world" (Matthew 28:20).

It is not I that live but Christ that lives in me

Christ said, "As ye have done it unto one of the least of these my brethren, ye have done it unto me" (Matthew 25:40). Read it literally. We did it to Christ because Christ was one with that individual. We must take the word of God more literally. Christ did not only become "us" but he became "me". Every person in this world has the right to say with apostle Paul "*I* am crucified with Christ, never the less I live, yet not I but Christ now liveth in *me*" (Galatians 2:20).

Now, if we will say that, for it is the truth of the matter if we will *let go and let God*, then is it just Christ that is living in me? It is more than the life of Christ. The Father lived and worked in Christ and so when we say that it is Christ that lives in me, we can say it is the Father that lives in me. "If a man love Me, he will keep my words: and My Father will love him, and We will come unto him, and make Our abode with him" (John 14:23). When the Father is working in Christ, He is working in us, then we also have a life that measures with the life of God for that life itself is the very life of God Himself.

The life of God without being God

But it must be made plain that we are not God, nor ever could be, for it is the lie of Satan that we "shall be as gods" (Genesis 3:5). Yet our life will be filled with the working of God. Imagine this. The life that Christ lived is the very life that God will live in us. A life of perfection. Freedom from the guilt of condemnation, for Christ in His death has borne that all away. A life where the divine mind has solved our problems and all we need to do is to let Him work that solution out. If He does the works, then He takes care of the consequences. If others don't like what He does through us, that's His problem, not ours. If they reject us, it is not we who they have rejected, but Him (Luke 10:16). We don't have to take it personally.

Adam in the garden of Eden could have lived a perfect life. Yet never could he have attained to so great a blessing as this; to have the very life of God itself lived through us! How can it be that one who is not God can live the life of God? Oh what wonder! What revelation. What privilege. What peace, comfort and joy.

Sinner, look at your life and confess the mess you have made of it. Be honest. Everything you touch falls apart, and everything else that doesn't, is a deception. Then look at the life of God and realise its perfect serenity can be yours if you will just stop trying to work things out yourself.

How, then, do I have this life? How did Christ have it? These questions we will now seek to answer.

CHAPTER 4

Christ was born of the Spirit

Jesus says, "Abide in Me and I in you for without Me ye can do nothing." But He of His own self could do nothing. The works that He did were not His own, but the works of the Father. Before we examine what it means to abide in Jesus Christ, let us first examine how it was that the Father abode in Him.

Firstly, it must be noticed that there was a difference in His birth as compared to our own. The angel said to Mary, "The Holy Ghost shall come upon thee, and the power of the Highest shall overshadow thee: therefore also that Holy Thing which shall be born of thee shall be called the Son of God" (Luke 1:35).

But whilst this Child was spoken of as "that Holy Thing", it must not be overlooked that He still received hereditary input from His mother Mary. Of what kind of a hereditary it was is clearly shown in the Old Testament and more especially identified in the accounts of the kings of Israel in the books of Kings and Chronicles. He did not receive anything "holy" from His mother.

It was the input from the Holy Ghost that supplied His holiness. Both at His birth, and the remainder of His life. His own words were, "The Father. . . dwelleth in me" (John 14:10). The indwelling of the Father was made possible by the presence of the Holy Spirit. It was by the Spirit that the Father dwelt within the bosom of His own Son.

This was no advantage above the rest of humanity, for we are called to be "born again", that we also might be "born of the Spirit". (John 3:5-8.) When we do this, just as the Father dwelt within His Son, so by being born again, the Spirit "dwelleth with you, and shall be in you" and, Jesus says, that by this means, "I will come to you." (John 14:17,18.) But more than this, "My Father will love him, and We will come unto him, and make our abode with him" (verse 21).

Except that Christ was born of the Spirit from birth, He entered fully into our own experience. And when we are born again of the Spirit of God, we too may begin our new life with a clean record, having all our past sins washed away so that we stand before God as a new man, as one who has never sinned. But the words "Holy Thing" can only ever apply to Christ because He is the only one who has lived a purely sinless existence.

How the Father lived in Christ

But how was it that the Father lived His life through His Son? We have a clue here in John 14:31 where Christ says, "As the Father gave me commandment, even so I do." The word "commandment" can be very confusing. We often read the word as something that we need to go and do. Shortly, we will arrive at a whole new appreciation of what this word actually means to us.

The Father gave Jesus the "commandment" and He did it. Elsewhere in the Gospels, Jesus says, "The Son can do nothing of Himself, but what He seeth the Father do: for what things so-ever He doeth, these also doeth the Son likewise. For the Father loveth the Son, and showeth Him all things that Himself doeth: and He will show Him greater works than these, that ye may marvel" (John 5:19, 20).

Here we can see an interesting interchange of words, but the same thought. Jesus did what the Father commanded Him to do; but how did He command Him? What He "seeth the Father do... these doeth the Son likewise... for the Father... showeth Him all things that Himself doeth." The same thought contained in giving the commandment is in the Father showing Him. The result was the same. The consequences were the obedience of the Father in the life of Christ.

The power of God is in His word

Let's find the synonymity in this thought. 2 Corinthians 4:6 tells us that God "commanded the light to shine out of darkness."

In Genesis 1:3 we read that God said, "Let there be light; and there was light." His word produced the thing itself. Again verse 9:

"And God said, Let the waters under the heaven be gathered together unto one place, and let the dry land appear: and it was so." Whatever God said, happened. He gave the commandment, "Let there be light", and "there was light." And this is how it was on each day of creation.

Isaiah 55:10-11 tells us, "For as the rain cometh down, and the snow from heaven, and returneth not thither, but watereth the earth, and maketh it bring forth and bud, that it may give seed to the sower, and bread to the eater: So shall my word be that goeth forth out of my mouth: it shall not return unto me void, but it shall accomplish that which I please, and it shall prosper in the thing whereto I sent it." The word of God is self-fulfilling. God speaks, and it is so. That is why God "cannot lie" (Titus 1:2).

When Jesus was tempted by Satan in the wilderness, He replied to each of Satan's suggestions with, "It is written." The word of God was His defence. In Psalm 119:11, He says, "Thy word have I hid in mine heart, that I might not sin against thee." And again in Psalms 17:4: "By the word of thy lips I have kept me from the paths of the destroyer." The power of God is in His word. Jesus Christ depended upon the word of God to keep Him from sinning.

Ephesians 6:17 describes the word as the "sword of the Spirit", and connecting that with Hebrews 4:12 we see that it is a mighty weapon in the battle against sin. Hebrews 4:12: "For the word of God is quick, and powerful, and sharper than any two-edged sword, piercing even to the dividing asunder of soul and spirit, and of the joints and marrow, and is a discerner of the thoughts and intents of the heart."

The word worked within Christ

As the Father gave the commandment, so Jesus did. The word that the Father gave worked within Him the keeping of the commandment. Speaking on behalf of Jesus in Psalm 40:7-8, the Psalmist writes, "Then said I, Lo, I come: in the volume of the book it is written of me, I delight to do thy will, O my God: yea, thy law is within my heart." The law of God was within the heart of Jesus, and through it, the Father worked His will in His Son's life.

Without faith, we cannot please God. When many of us read of His ten commandments, we read of them as instructions as something that we have to go and do, and if we do not do them, then we are condemned to death. But we need to make the connection between God commanding the light to shine out of darkness and God commanding His law from Sinai. In Genesis, the commandment itself produced what it desired. And God is "the same yesterday, and to day, and for ever" (Hebrews 13:8). His word will always work *if* we will do that which creation did in the beginning – "let".

Ten promises

2 Peter 1:4 tells us that God has "given unto us exceeding great and precious promises: that by these ye might be partakers of the divine nature, having escaped the corruption that is in the world through lust." This especially includes the ten commandments. To those who possess genuine faith, ten commandments cease to be an arbitrary rule, but rather witnesses to the "righteousness of God" which is manifested in the life of "all them that believe" (Romans 3:21, 22).

Jesus Christ understood the power of the word. And He submitted Himself to its influence. In the Old Testament, the Father showed Him what He was doing. To the believers in the upper room after His resurrection, Christ "said unto them, These are the words which I spake unto you, while I was yet with you, that all things must be fulfilled, which were written in the law of Moses, and in the prophets, and in the psalms, concerning Me" (Luke 24:44). In the law of Moses, in the Prophets, and in the Psalms, the Father had showed His Son what it was that He would work within Him and at what time. To the two heart-broken disciples on the road to Emmaus, "beginning at Moses and all the prophets, He expounded unto them in all the scriptures the things concerning Himself" (Luke 24:27.) The entire Old Testament was the revelation of the life that the Father would live in His own Son when He sent Him here to this earth. And as Christ studied that word with a heart receptive to its influence, when the fulness of time was come, the Father wrought through His word.

In the following chapter, we shall look at the faith of Jesus that brought to Him the working of the word.

CHAPTER 5

The power of God unto salvation

Jesus did not "live by bread only, but by every word that proceedeth out of the mouth of the Lord" (Deuteronomy 8:3). Daily He submitted to the working of the word in His life. That word was "the power of God unto salvation" (Romans 1:16). He knew that it was by the "power of His word" that God was "upholding all things" (Hebrews 1:3), and He trusted that if that power was able to keep the worlds in their orderly motion, and to stay the sun in its morning and evening course, it could be trusted to keep Him from falling into sin.

But there was something in particular about Jesus' belief in the power of God. In James 2:19 it tells us that "the devils also believe, and tremble." The devils understand the power of God. They know it by first-hand experience. They have witnessed the creation of a thousand worlds. They also believe that God so loved the world that He sent His Son into this world. They believe many things of which the Scriptures declare concerning God. They also know that there is power in His word to accomplish what He says. Yet they are not saved. Therefore they tremble, knowing that His word which declares judgement against evildoers will be fulfilled. Many Christians today believe the love of God that sent His Son to die for them. They believe that His word is true; that His promises are sure; that the destruction He warns us of is imminent, yet they seem to come short of living a life as pure and holy as that of the Son of God. Why is this? What was so special about the faith of Jesus that brought into His life the obedience of God?

Christ read the word of God as speaking to Himself

It was simply this: He read the word of God as speaking to Himself personally. He didn't take any of the scriptures and say, "Oh, that refers to someone else." No. He took each word and applied it to Himself personally. In short, when He read in the word of God: "Thou art the man", He took it as – that means me.

When Jesus Christ hung upon the cross, He cried out, "My God, My God, why has thou forsaken Me?" In Isaiah 59:1-2 it explains His experience. "Behold, the Lord's hand is not shortened, that it cannot save; neither his ear heavy, that it cannot hear: But your iniquities have separated between you and your God, and your sins have hid His face from you, that He will not hear." Christ was meeting the fulfilment of Isaiah 53, that "the Lord hath laid on Him the iniquity of us all" (vs 6). Under this load of guilt which He bore for us, He declares, "But I am a worm, and no man" (Psalm 22:6). "For innumerable evils have compassed Me about: Mine iniquities have taken hold upon Me, so that I am not able to look up; they are more than the hairs of Mine head: therefore my heart faileth Me" (Psalm 40:12).

Jesus submitted Himself to all the terrible sins that had been identified in the Scriptures. To each and every accusation of the word of God against evildoers, He said, "I am that man."

He took the promises personally

Likewise, He claimed the promises of God and applied them to His own personal experience. In Psalm 22 the awful prophet- ic cry is made, "My God, my God, why hast thou forsaken Me? why art thou so far from helping Me, and from the words of My roaring?. . . All they that see Me laugh Me to scorn: they shoot out the lip, they shake the head, saying, He trusted on the Lord that He would deliver Him: let Him deliver Him, seeing He delighted in Him. . . For dogs have compassed Me: the assembly of the wicked have enclosed Me: they pierced My hands and My feet. I may tell all My bones: they look and stare upon Me. They part My garments among them, and cast lots upon My vesture." (verses 1,7,8,16-18)

But chapter 23 is the Shepherd Psalm. "The Lord is my shepherd; I shall not want. He maketh Me to lie down in green pastures: He leadeth Me beside the still waters. He restoreth my soul: He leadeth Me in the paths of righteousness for His name's sake." Christ had never strayed from the path of right-doing. He had ever done the will of His Father, and now, even though He cannot see His reconciling face, He believes and trusts that the Father is still His tender, caring shepherd, and that even now, upon the cross, He was leading Him in the path of righteousness.

Jesus was in the valley of the shadow of death, and the word to Him at that time was, "Yea, though I walk through the valley of the shadow of death, I will fear no evil: for thou art with Me; Thy rod and Thy staff they comfort Me." He received this as a promise to Himself that even though the gulf between Him and His Father was so broad, so black, so deep, "Thou art with Me." And He said, "Father, into thy hands I commend my spirit: and having said thus, he gave up the ghost" (Luke 23:46). He trusted the words "Thou art with Me" and commended Himself into the hands of the Father whom He believed was right beside Him in the darkness.

Jesus Himself is declared to be the Word of God. As His life departed from Him, He rested in the promise that on the third day He would come forth from the tomb glorified. "For thou wilt not leave my soul in hell; neither wilt thou suffer thine Holy One to see corruption" (Psalm 16:10.) He trusted that God would keep His Word.

"Thou preparest a table before Me in the presence of Mine enemies: Thou anointest My head with oil; My cup runneth over. Surely goodness and mercy shall follow Me all the days of My life: and I will dwell in the house of the Lord for ever" (Psalm 23:5-5).

Psalm 24 is the ascension Psalm. Verses 7-10: "Lift up your heads, O ye gates; and be ye lift up, ye everlasting doors; and the King of glory shall come in. Who is this King of glory? The Lord strong and mighty, the Lord mighty in battle. Lift up your heads, O ye gates; even lift them up, ye everlasting doors; and the King of glory shall come in. Who is this King of glory? The Lord of hosts, He is the King of glory."

The faith of Jesus

Christ received the Scriptures as speaking of Himself personally. And day by day, the Father unfolded to Him His will, like turning from page to page. From that which He realised at the first Passover in Jerusalem, that His life would be given for the sins of the world, through to riding on the colt at His triumphal entrance, and then Gethsemane to Calvary, each moment of His life was a submission to the wonderful working of the word of God as He took it and applied it to Himself personally.

And such a faith brought to Him the obedience of God. This is the faith of Jesus.

CHAPTER 6

The same privilege is offered to us

Christ did not live His own life. Rather, He yielded moment by moment to the life of the Father. It was not Christ that was manifest in humanity, but the Father Himself. Christ had laid down His own self – He "humbled Himself" (Philippians 2:8) – and it was the Father who did the works in Him.

There is nothing that we can do of our own selves that will cause us to deserve eternal life. All that we can do is defiled by sin. It doesn't matter how perfect our imitation of God's own character is as exemplified by the Ten Commandments, the truth is that all our "right doings are as filthy rags" (Isaiah 64:6). Therefore God is offering us the same privilege – that is, to have the Father Himself live His own life through us.

Christ is our example

Christ partook of our own condition and situation. He Himself says, "I can of Mine own self do nothing" (John 5:30). Having laid His own self down, and taken ourselves upon Him, He makes the declaration on behalf of us all, "We can of our own selves do nothing." This is the initial point where our personal experience with Jesus Christ commences. We must make the same confession. Christ was baptized – not because of His sins, for He had none – but to be an example for us; to show that we must commence our new life in Him by laying the old life down by the confession that "I cannot" and "I have not". Our acknowledgement of our condition must be sincere and not just lip service. It must come from a heart that is crushed by sin and sees that everything it has ever performed in this life was in vain. "Except the Lord build the house, they that build it labour in vain" (Psalm 127:1).

A broken spirit and a contrite heart is God's own sacrifice

Too often we have taken things into our own hands and not waited for God to come through for us. Like King Saul, we grow impatient and perform the sacrifice ourselves. How often do we think that it is our own broken spirit and contrite heart that God will not despise (Psalm 51:17). But no, that is not what the Scripture is meaning. Indeed, He will not despise the broken spirit and contrite heart, for He says, "The heaven is My throne and the earth is My footstool" (Isaiah 66:1) – I have made all these things, yet I will not look to them – they have not my love and adoration, "but to this man will I look, even to him that is poor and of a contrite spirit, and trembleth at my word" (Isaiah 66:1-2). The broken spirit and contrite heart which He will not despise is *His own sacrifice*, and this He supplied in His Son. This is the sacrifice which He will not despise, and only as we share with Jesus Christ in *His* broken state, confessing our utter inability to do anything right without the Father's doing it for us, only then will we have the approbation of God.

That which issues out of the heart of God

It is His Son who was obedient to the Father His whole entire life. The rest of us fall short of the glory of God. Our salvation is only through Christ. But only as we are constantly reaching out for it in Him will we find it. Our sense of desperation must be so great that we will fear to live our own life and day by day, moment by moment, cry out, "You do it Lord, because I can't."

The Father produced His own life in His Son through the working of the word within Him. In the beginning when God spoke, the word spoken was the product of His own heart. "God saw everything that he had made, and, behold, it was very good" (Genesis 1:31). Out of the heart are the issues of life. God's heart is pure, and holy and good, and that which He spoke into existence in the beginning of creation was exactly that. And the word of God produced the very thing of which He spoke.

When Jesus Christ was on the road to Emmaus, He showed the two disciples "in all the scriptures the things concerning Himself"

(Luke 24:27). The entire Old Testament was a revelation of the life of Christ. But that life that He lived was the life of the Father.

The flesh and blood of Christ

The night before the crucifixion, Christ instituted the ordinance service of the bread and the wine. Most likely unknown to them, Christ had sought to help His disciples understand the meaning of this in His conversation with the people the day after the feeding of the five thousand (John 6). He had declared to them that eternal life could only be gained by drinking His blood and eating His flesh. The writings of Moses had forbidden them to eat blood, and they were repulsed and indignant at what they thought to be cannibalism.

Christ proceeded to clarify His statement for those that were spiritually discerning and He stated that the words that He spoke were what would give them life. The people were to receive His words and to assimilate them into their experience. He was not speaking of His literal flesh and blood.

While much of the Christian world acknowledges the blood of Christ which "cleanseth us from all sin" (1 John 1:7), they see it only as shed upon the cross at Calvary – the death of the sacrificial victim for the sins of the whole world. Yet the "life... is in the blood" (Leviticus 17:11). When the scriptures speak of the blood of Christ, they are not just referring to His death. While the death of Christ upon the cross reconciles us to God, it is the *life* of Christ which saves us (Romans 5:10). And this life is that which was in the blood. By partaking of the *life* of Christ, we will be saved. When we are crucified with Christ, our past sins are washed away. It is sin that separates us from God. When that sin is all gone, there is nothing to separate us from God and we are "reconciled to God" (Romans 5:10); yet this only deals with the sin that has been committed. What about the potential to commit it again? This is dealt with by the life of Christ, for as we receive His life, we receive the same victory over the temptation and tendencies to evil that He gained.

The word is the life

A highly important connecting thought is that Christ declared the words that He speaks to be spirit and life (John 6:63). Christ said, "Man shall not live by bread alone, but by every word that proceedeth out of the mouth of God" (Matthew 4:4). The word itself is life-giving for "by the word of the Lord were the heavens made. . . for he spake, and it was done; he commanded, and it stood fast (Psalm 33:6, 9). "And God said, Let there be light: and there was light" (Genesis 1:3). Therefore the life of Christ is in the word, and as we receive the word and its power to work within us, we receive the life of Christ. But more than this, as it was the Father who worked in Christ through the word, it is the life of the Father Himself that is in the word. Even though it was Christ that led the Israelites in the wilderness, and He who spoke with and through the prophets, the same subservience that Christ manifested to the Father when He walked this earth is manifested in the Old Testament. When He declared Himself to be self-existent and eternal, He said, "The Lord God, and his Spirit, hath sent me." Christ Himself is the Word (John 1), yet even in the Old Testament, the Son spoke not by Himself, but was expressing the Father's own thoughts. Hence it is the life of the Father that is manifest in the Old Testament and this is the life which He lived in Christ. What love does Christ have for us that He would lay His own self down and become subservient to Him who was His equal in all things!

Building upon this foundation of truth, when we study both the Old and New Testament Scriptures, we are reading of the life of Christ. This same life we are to make our own – to ingest it and assimilate it. But how do we do this?

CHAPTER 7

Reading ourselves into the word

When we read the Bible, we must see that the entire Scriptures are speaking of Christ. The Old Testament is a revelation of what the Father *would* work in Him, and the New Testament reveals what the Father *did* work in Him, but not only in Him, but also in the lives of all those who received these truths, such as Apostle Paul. We ourselves must also read the Scriptures as speaking of our own selves. All of the warnings and all of the promises in the Scriptures are for us. But only do they benefit us as we read ourselves into the biblical accounts.

Let me illustrate. The harlot Mary was thrown at the feet of Jesus for her condemnation. But Christ declared, "Neither do I condemn thee. Go and sin no more" (John 8:11). While there is an abundance of hope for us in this revelation of Christ's love for us in not condemning us for our sins, the blessing of this story is only half received. Reading the word of God in a very literal sense, we see that this special promise is for those who are guilty of harlotry and adultery. Is it not true that those whose lives contain such histories find the greatest comfort in these words? But this comfort is available to all of us, for each one of us are no better than anyone else. Except it be for the Holy Spirit that restrains us, how many of us would be guilty of the same sins as whom the Pharisees condemned! The Bible declares that the works of *the* flesh (singular) are manifest. This means that we all have the same potential. Certain sinful tendencies are stronger in some than in others, and are dependent upon our genetics and cultivated habits, yet the same propensity resides within us all. And it may not necessarily take much for it to come to the surface.

When we are willing to acknowledge this, and confess ourselves the chief of sinners (1 Timothy 1:15), then we will not be ashamed of counting all experiences in the Scriptures as our own.

Yea, rather, we will even esteem everyone else, even the vilest sinner, better than ourselves (Philippians 2:3). But the point in hand is this: When the prophet Nathan came to David declaring, "Thou art the man" (2 Samuel 12:7), we will make the same confession as David and say, "I am the man." We will consider our own selves as guilty of murder and adultery. I will confess that this is a hard thing to do, for I experience the difficulty of it in my own self, yet when I do this, the promise is mine. Christ says to the adulterer, "Neither do I condemn thee. Go and sin no more." And to the murderer David, the promise is mine also: "The Lord also hath put away thy sin" (2 Samuel 12:13). God is very specific, and when dealing with Him, we must be specific also.

But some may say, "I am not guilty of murder." Have you ever been angry with a family member or a friend? Christ declares that this is murder (Matthew 5:21-22), for the truthfulness of the matter is that if you had the opportunity, you would have removed them from the world. You may say, "I have not committed adultery." Have you ever looked upon a woman or a man and thought about having sex with them? (See Matthew 5:28). I know there may be some who will say, "Never have I done these things in all my life!" Then you, especially, must account yourself as being guilty of the same as every sinner in the Bible, none excepted.

Never try to hide your sins from God

We should never be ashamed of confessing our sins, even though they may only remain in the realm of our thoughts, for God knows them all already. There is nothing we can hide from Him. In fact, there is great relief found in confessing our sins and acknowledging our errors. If God already knows what we have done, then why try to hide it from Him, and needlessly bear the sense of its guilt upon our conscience? Why not just say, "Lord, I'm sorry. I sinned." If we will do that, it is gone, all gone. For when the Spirit of God convicts us that something is sinful, and we will confess that that is so, our sins will be gone. For to confess is to say the same thing – "It is sin" and "if we confess our sins, He is faithful and just to forgive us our sins, and to cleanse us from all" unrighteousness" (1 John 1:9).

Christ took the blame for all our sins and confessed them even though He never committed them

Jesus Christ Himself confessed to every sin that every man and woman who ever lived ever committed. And He was not guilty of a single one! The Psalmist reveals what was going through Christ's mind as He hung upon the cross. He says, "My sins are more than the hairs of my head" and, "My sins are not hid from Thee" (Psalm 40:12; 69:5). Christ counted *all sins* as His own. So perfectly did He identify Himself as having committed each terrible act that He suffered the *guilt* of those sins. "The Lord hath laid on Him the iniquity of us all." The cry that was rent from the lips of Christ, "My God, my God, why hast Thou forsaken Me?" (Psalm 22:1; Matthew 27:46) is a terrible testimony to the reality of the real burden of guilt that Christ bore. For in Isaiah it says, "Your sins have hid His face from you, that He will not hear" (Isaiah 59:2). Christ further says in the Psalms, "Why art Thou so far from helping Me, and from the words of My roaring?" (Psalm 22:1). It was because of our own sins which were made to be His own. They really did become His own and Christ literally bore the punishment for every sin that has ever been committed. He died not from His wounds, but from a heart broken and smashed by the weight of our sins that separated Him from His Father.

We also must confess all

This also is to be our experience. For we are to be "crucified with Christ" and buried with Him "in the likeness of His death" (Galatians 2:20; Romans 6:5). It is this broken spirit and contrite heart that God will not despise. It is the broken heart of a sinner who will be as the thief beside Christ upon the cross saying, "Lord, remember me." The thief looked at his life and saw that it all resulted in his present desperate experience. Christ looked at His own life, and saw all of humanity that He had gathered into His bosom and saw only that which destroys the soul. We also must look at our lives, at ourselves, and confess that "in me. . . dwelleth no good thing", "no, not one" (Romans 3:12; 7:18); that I deserve eternal destruction, and that all the fires of hell, though they raged forever, could not punish me according to my guilt.

The "Acceptable Time"

But Christ knew the time when the human soul is most "acceptable" with God, for He had demonstrated it to many during His ministry. At the bottom of life's pit, the weight of the sins of the whole world weighing heavily upon Him, feeling as though He were "a worm and no man" (Psalm 22:6), and that His sins were more heavy than the hairs of His head so that He could not look up (Psalm 40:12), He cries from His heart, "My prayer is unto Thee, O Lord, in an *acceptable time*: O God, in the multitude of thy mercy hear Me" (Psalm 69:13).

In Isaiah 49:7-8 we read the response of the Father's heart at this time. "Thus saith the Lord. . . to Him whom man despiseth, to Him whom the nation abhorreth. . . in an *acceptable time* have I heard thee, and in a day of salvation have I helped thee: and I will preserve thee, and give thee for a covenant of the people." It is when we fall all broken at the foot of the cross upon which Christ is hanging that we are acceptable in God's sight. God knows that we cannot live our lives right. He knows that we only ever make a mess of everything and that everything we touch will eventually fall apart. He is waiting for us to admit this, to be honest and tell Him how sorry we are that we have tried to work things out ourselves. And gazing upon Christ upon the cross, bearing the same guilt that we bear, suffering the penalty for the sins that we have committed, and yet seeing that He willingly receives this punishment on our behalf for our own sake, our own self-glory is laid in the dust. Knowing the love of God for a sinner who confesses His guilt, and that the Father was right there beside Him at the cross, Jesus says, "Into thy hands I commend my Spirit" (Luke 23:46). He knew that God would receive a broken spirit and a contrite heart – for it was His own sacrifice. And He bowed His head upon His breast and gave up the ghost. So we too may rest in the same love and cast our own broken hearts before the Father, crying, "Into Thy hands I commend my spirit." And the peace of Christ as He rested in the grave will be our own also.

This is the beginning of our salvation. And the Alpha is also the Omega (Revelation 21:6).

I die daily

In the words of Apostle Paul, "I die daily" (1 Corinthians 15:31), is the description of the new life in Christ. If we died with Him, then we will rise again with Him. As He took our sinful life upon Himself and bore it to an eternal grave, then His own life will now be ours in exchange. And what was His life? A life filled with the working of the Father, acceptable both unto God and to the law. Therefore our own life will be filled with the working of the Father and free from guilt and condemnation.

Christ received the word as speaking of Himself. And we must do the same if we would bear the same fruit in our own lives.

CHAPTER 8

Christ became one with every individual

All scriptures speak of Christ. But they also speak of us. How can this be? For we are not God, neither are we the word of God. Christ was the word, and "the word was with God and was God... and without Him was not anything made that was made" (John 1:1-3). We, on the other hand, are mere mortals worthy of eternal damnation. Yet that Word was "made flesh and dwelt among us" (John 1:14). Yeah, more than among us, for Christ says that He has become at one with us and that whatsoever we do unto others we do it unto Him (Matthew 25:40). That "among" is not to be only an external experience, but an internal one also. Christ declared that whatsoever we do unto the least of these His brethren (and He called all men His brethren (Hebrews 2:17)), we do it unto Him. How can this be? Only if He became one with the individual.

Likewise with the words of Hebrews that Christ was made in all things like unto His brethren. "All things" does not exclude anything. He is identical with ourselves. Only if He is in all things like as we are can He be touched with the feeling of our infirmities and be tempted in all things even as we are. And when we are tempted, we are tempted in different ways, so that Christ must be tempted as an individual with the individual.

Except Christ became ourselves He could not save us

To apply this thought to life's experiences is the eating of Christ's flesh and drinking His blood. Christ is one with every individual, therefore He could claim the guilt of every individual and stand before God's law as having committed the transgression. The law of God will not permit a substitute. Indeed, the law of the land would not do so, and God's law is "holy, and just, and good" (Romans 7:12). Therefore, in order for Christ to take the sins of the whole world upon Himself, He needed to become every individual sinner. And therefore, Christ is one with you and me both personally and individually.

How else could He understand my temptation today? And how else can He make atonement for my sins before God, pleading His own life in my stead before a law that requires a perfect obedience from the specific individual? How could He do all this two thousand years since He walked the earth? Only by becoming one with you and me on an individual basis, so perfectly identified with ourselves that as the law looks upon Him, it sees us. Only by Him becoming ourselves and placing us behind His back and bearing the brunt of the wrath against transgression can He really be our Saviour. For except Christ became ourselves, He could not save us. If we would live eternally, there must be a perfect life, specifically our own, that can be presented before the law and its requirements; a perfect existence beginning right from the very day that we were born, for the wages of sin is death and if there is any trace of sin in our lives, we will die an eternal death.

When He died we died

Christ died this eternal death for us. Yet as He was one with us, when He died, we died. And this dying experience should be a daily experience – one that is moment by moment. If we will do this, then the life that Christ lives will be our very own life and when reading of Christ in the Scriptures, we really will be reading of ourselves. The Apostle Paul declared all this in his wonderful words, "For I am crucified with Christ, nevertheless I live, yet not I but the life that I now life in the flesh I live by the faith of the Son of God who loved me and gave Himself for me" (Galatians 2:20).

Christ was one with me

The very same life that Christ lived will be my very own. For indeed, He perfectly identified Himself with me. What the Father worked in Him, He worked in me. And it worked in you. Two thousand years ago is a mini display of the life that Christ has lived for each and every one of us. Yes, His life was full of much suffering and we will partake of His sufferings, but we will also be partakers of His joy. Besides, His sufferings were only for the salvation of man and for glorifying God in heaven. These are truly worthy reasons for suffering, and that which we will experience will be nothing compared with an eternal weight of glory (2 Corinthians 4:17). Even in the midst of it all, Jesus had peace, and He promises that the same peace will be ours, a peace which passes all understanding (Philippians 4:7).

How can we have peace in a world of so much sin? Aaaah, because it is not our own life that we live. We have not a care in the world, for it is God that "careth for you" (1 Peter 5:7) and we need not bother ourselves with stressing about what we shall eat or wear, etc., for God knows we have need of these things and He is the one that makes provision. Just seek His kingdom, He says, and His own right-doing in your life and He will take care of the rest (Matthew 6:31-33).

The Holy Spirit will show us our future life

When trouble comes upon us, as it surely will, for Christ prayed that we not be taken from the world but kept from the world (John 17:11), we are not left alone. The Holy Spirit will take of Jesus and show Him unto us (John 16:13-15). He will show us Christ dying upon the cross in consequence for our sins, and painfully identify the very thing in our hearts that put Him there. He will show us the perfect life that Christ has lived on our behalf and now offers to give to each and every one of us. And He may permit judgments and calamities to warn us back from the brink of grieving Him should we turn away from this great and most precious gift, or grasp it with only a feeble and desperate-less hand. (John 16:7-8.)

He will also show us things to come (John 16:13). He will show us what the future holds for us; that "we must through much tribulation enter into the kingdom of God" (Acts 14:22), and all that live the godly life of Christ Jesus will suffer persecution (2 Timothy 3:12). But it is important to note that it is when He shows us Jesus that He is showing us things to come. This is because Christ's life is my own life. And what God was doing in Him, He was doing in me. And what He has done in Him, He has done in me. All I need to do is *let* it be my reality.

Christ promised that the faithful ones would be taken before kings and courts and will have to testify for their faith (Matthew 10:17-18). Was not this Christ's experience also? He stood firmly and unflinchingly before Annas, Caiaphas and Pilate as you and as me. When He did it, we did it. And when we go through it, we will only be living the life that Christ has already lived; we also will stand firmly and unflinchingly before kings and priests and rulers.

Christ rested in His Father's love during the storm and so can we

One favourite story of mine is Christ sleeping in the stern of the boat upon the stormy sea. Oh how life is so much like this at times – truly more times than we would hope! Yet Christ was at peace, while everyone around Him was in distress (Luke 8:23-25). The disciples did all that they could in their own strength to save themselves, yet all their efforts availed nothing. Christ, on the other hand, rested in the Father's love. He knew that "all things work together for good to them that love God, to them who are the called according to his purpose" (Romans 8:28) and that there was a purpose in it all, and He waited in quiet submission to when God Himself would bring deliverance. Truly Christ's patience caused a great suffering to the disciples, but had they also rested in the Father's care, they would have been like the Apostle Paul on his way to Rome, who, although shipwrecked, feared not for his life, but accepted all that which providence would suffer him to experience for his own salvation and the salvation of others. It was not Christ, but the Father that stilled the sea that moonlit night. And it was the peaceful life of Christ that Paul had received that spoke the words of faith and encouragement that dreadful night that saved the lives of all. (See Acts 27 for the story of Paul.)

To believe is to receive the life of Christ as my own

To believe is to receive. If we truly believe the wonderful truth that the life that Christ lived is my very own life, and that when I read of Him I am reading of myself, then I will receive that life, and it will be my own in a very practical sense. And as God worked in Him by the word, so it will produce the same life in ourselves.

CHAPTER 9

Abraham's belief

The original meaning of the word *believe* implies submission. To believe is to receive; but to receive what? To receive the influence of the life of Christ as that to which we are to submit. The Old Testament word for believe is *amen*, which simply means, "Let it be so". This was the kind of belief that Abraham had. He believed God and this was accounted to Him for righteousness. This is not just in the sense of a legal transaction, as in *justification*, but in practical reality. Abraham yielded to God's promise – to the power that was in His word – and therefore his works witnessed as to what kind of belief he had. True believing is yielding to and trusting God's word to do exactly what it says. If God declared Abraham to be righteous this must mean that the very works of Abraham themselves must have been a product of God. And therefore Abraham could not have been in any dispensation different to the one in which the Christian world is in today, for his own belief was identical to that which our own must be.

Abraham was declared to be the "Friend of God" (James 2:23). Why is this? Amos 3:3 provides the simple answer: "How can two walk together unless they be agreed?" Abraham and God were in complete agreement. Their relationship was what ours with God should be. What God said, Abraham agreed with, he said "Amen!" and he let it be so. And thus their lives were in perfect harmony because they were the same life.

The promised child could not be born until Abraham's faith received God's word

There was a time when he did not say, "Amen," and took God's promise into his own hands. For a moment, his faith failed and he tried to solve the problem himself. Perhaps if it wasn't for his own wife's weak faith, he may have endured, but giving in to the temptation, he took things into his own hands. He was growing old and his aged wife could not bear any children. Yet God had promised that he would have an heir. Forgetting the power of God, he acted upon his wife's advice and slept with her maidservant Hagar. (Genesis 16.)

Hagar fell pregnant and a child was born. Yet God returned to Abraham saying that he would yet have a son through his wife, Sarah. Upon hearing this, Sarah laughed for she was now much older than when the promise was first made. Bearing Christ's reproof with a humble spirit, she believed and bore a son to Abraham in the following year.

The trial of Abraham's faith is the same for us today. It was not the birth of an heir that he was worried about, although this was also dear to his heart. What he desired the most was for- giveness for his sins and peace with God through the sacrifice of Christ. And he knew he could only have this as his own life would be one with the life of Christ. Yet Christ had not yet taken upon Himself humanity; the promise of the woman's seed crushing the serpent's head had not yet been fulfilled and Abraham was one in a long line of patriarchs who hoped that through their own posterity, Jesus the Christ, the seed of the woman, would be born.

The promise to Abraham was that this blessing for the whole world would come through his own posterity. Were Abraham to have no children, then Christ could not be born. Of course, the word that had proceeded from God's mouth would not return unto Him void, but it had to wait upon Abraham's belief, or else it would work in another manner and Abraham would be deprived of the blessing. Abraham had received the promise personally, and considered that if he had no son, then he had no redeemer. This was the motivating force in his actions.

Abraham at first believed with all his heart and was counted as righteous. But a sojourn in the idolatrous Egypt seems to have dulled his faith and the faith of his wife. His marriage with Hagar brought only contempt and distress to his home, and Abraham and Sarah greatly regretted their actions. They saw that by trying to save themselves, they had only messed things up, and apparently made matters worse and the promise almost impossible; for they were now much older.

Christ came to Abraham as himself

God did not abandon Abraham in his distress. He received the confession of the husband and wife and visited them to renew the promise. His manner of visiting with them was of uttermost importance, for us today also. The faith of Abraham was set upon a Redeemer who could plead on his behalf before a perfect law. He knew that only by being the woman's seed – issuing from the very fountainhead of sin, for the woman was first in the transgression – could Christ ever be his Saviour. Abraham saw himself also as a fountain head of sin for he knew that there was no good thing in his life that he could do and that every time he tried to work things out, he only made things worse. Christ knew the thoughts of his soul that kept him so meek and humble and yet strong in God's power and at the time of repeating the promise, He comforted him by the display of evidence that the promise would be fulfilled.

One warm day, three strangers approached the tent of Abraham. As was his habit, he ran to meet them and invited them to his home for home for refreshments. Christ himself was in the trio. Yet how did He appear to Abraham? In the form of a humble sojourner, wearied and dusty from His travels. Abraham himself never received a foot of the inheritance in his life; he was a sojourner in the land. Christ appeared to him at one with him in his life's experience. This was evidence that the promise would be fulfilled and Christ would be born of a woman. Especially was it evidence that Abraham was one with His redeemer, for the great I AM is also "the Lamb slain from before the foundation of the world" (Revelation 13:8). Abraham's faith was strengthened; Isaac was born and when he was asked to offer him up as a sacrifice, he flinched not, but counted that God would raise him up again (Hebrews 11:19), for he knew and doubted not that the I AM would be born of Isaac's line and he would be one with all humanity.

Christ met Joshua as himself

The Bible provides other evidences of Christ's perfect identification with each one of us. As Moses' successor, Joshua, crossed over the Jordan, he beheld the great walls of Jericho and wondered how they might be overcome. As captain of the great host of Israelites, a heavy burden of responsible faith weighed upon his shoulders. Stepping aside from the encampment to seek the Lord, he was approached by a large warrior with a sword in his hand. Asking him whether he was for them or against them, the strange warrior, Christ Himself, answered, "I am the captain of the Lord's host..." (Joshua 5:14). Again Christ meets with the desperate individual as one with himself. Joshua had been a mighty warrior and fought many battles under Moses' guidance. And now he bore his role as captain of the Lord's host. Christ met him as one with himself.

Christ shared the experience with Shadrach, Meshach, and Abednego

Upon the plain of Dura in the province of Babylon, King Nebuchadnezzar erected a large, golden statue and commanded that all the representatives of his vast kingdom bow down and worship it. Among them were three friends who refused the command and these were reported to the king. These men were brought be- fore him and the enraged Nebuchadnezzar offered them another chance, yet at their admission that they would do the same again, the king cast them into a burning, fiery furnace. The flames were so hot that the men who threw them in were killed by the heat. But the three were untouched by the fire and all that burned was the ropes that bound their hands. Astonished, King Nebuchad- nezzar rose to his feet, and, gazing into the furnace, he saw not three but four men in the fire. Christ was one with his servants in their trials and afflictions. (Daniel 3.)

Jacob meets his equal

One most powerful example of Christ's unity with each and every one of us is the story of Jacob. As many of us experience, the time came when he had to meet the deeds of his past – the "skeletons in the closet", as they call them. Returning from twenty years in exile, with wives and children and great flocks and herds in tow, he is informed that the brother whom he had so greatly offended is approaching with a large group of armed warriors. Fearing for his life, he does all in his power to appease his brother's wrath, yet not feeling that this was sufficient, he departs to the river Jabbok to spend the night pleading with God for deliverance from the consequences of his own foolishness of many years before.

The river runs by and the shadows of the trees engulf him as he bows upon his knees pouring out his desperate heart before God. Suddenly a hand is laid upon his shoulder and he thinks that he is being attacked by an enemy. He fears for his life and wrestles with his antagonist in the dark shadows of the night. He was a strong man, one who had proved himself mighty in combat, for when talking with his wives father, he declares that when the roving bands came, and also the wild beasts, he drove them all away. He does not relent in the fight, yet he is surprised by the strength of the one against whom he struggles. At no time in his life has he met such a combatant, one who is equal in strength and skill to himself. They wrestle on through the cold hours of the night, neither gaining the upper hand over the other but so perfectly matched in skill and strength that one cannot gain the ascendancy over the other. All the while, ignorant of who his opponent is, Jacob pours out his heart to God declaring that all is as he deserves, yet would not God accept his repentance from twenty years earlier when he first awakened to his sin? Exhausted, he fights on, not willing to lose in the combat and hoping that deliverance from this foe and his brother will yet be given him from a merciful and pitiful God.

As the day breaks and the dawn begins to gild the skies, the stranger with whom he had wrestled all night touches Jacob's thigh and it is instantly dislocated. Jacob falls to the ground, yet not overcome. Realizing that He with whom he had fought was the very one to whom he had been pleading deliverance, he holds Him fast saying, "I will not let Thee go except Thou bless me" (Genesis 32:26). The blessing is granted and Jacob is given a new name because he prevailed with man and with God.

Who was it that wrestled with him? It was Christ Himself. But He could not overcome, neither could He be overcome. Why not?

Because He had made Himself equal to Jacob. His strength and skill was identical because He had become one with him.

Their Saviour is our Saviour

This is the Saviour whom the patriarchs worshipped and this is the Saviour we must worship; or else Christ is no Saviour to us. The same manner in which He has manifested Himself to desperate saints, He will manifest Himself to us today. He invites us to receive His word, to take it personally and believe that Christ has become one with us.

No, neither He nor we lose our individuality – He is still Christ and we are not Him; but as He is one with the Father, and therefore "God", He is one with us and therefore "John" or "Peter" or "Paul". Where the Holy Spirit is, there is Christ, and where Christ is, the Father is there also (John 14:23).

Could it be that a great secret has been kept from us for many, many years? Oh how many people sink to the grave in utter despair and desperation, never fully realising the great gift that God has prepared for every one of us. A new life! Our very own, yet filled with God's own perfection.

The devil has had great success in hiding this truth from our eyes and hearts. But it will no longer remain in the darkness. God has promised that it will lighten the whole earth with its glory. He has promised that the mystery will be finished, the mystery that hath been hid through eternal ages but now made manifest which is "Christ in you, the hope of glory" (Colossians 1:26-27).

Christ as you – hope indeed!

CHAPTER 10

What it means to "know" Christ

Jeremiah declares that God is married unto us (Jeremiah 3:14). Genesis describes marriage as the union of two person into "one flesh" (Genesis 2:24). It is the consummation of the marriage on the night of the wedding that unites the two persons into one. "And Adam knew Eve his wife; and she conceived, and bare Cain" (Genesis 4:1). The word "knew" or "know" denotes the close and personal intimacy between the husband and wife. Although the marriage relation falls short of illustrating the close union of Christ with every person individually, Christ's words to those who boasted in their own works, "I never knew you" (Matthew 7:21-23), indicates that these individuals never entered into a personal relationship with Him. He had been knocking at their heart's door, desiring to come into them and share their life's experiences (Revelation 3:20), but they chose to live their own lives without Him. Therefore He says, "Depart from Me, ye that work iniquity" (Matthew 7:23). Their works were their own works; their faith did not bring them that life that was full of God's own working (Romans 14:23).

Receiving the heart of Christ

Ezekiel states that God will write His law in our hearts and in our minds. Christ came declaring that the law of God was in His heart and that He delighted in His will. When we become one with Christ and let go of our old life and receive the new, we will receive Christ's very own heart as our own. He will take away our cold and stony service of rendering to the Lord an "all that the Lord hath said will we do" (Exodus 19:8; 24:7), and we will receive the very heart of Christ, a living heart, soft and subdued, molded by the Father as the potter molds the clay (Isaiah 64:8).

The Apostle Peter

The dear, but proud Peter wept at the very place where Christ had wept. He realised that Christ had read his soul because He shared the same soul with himself. Tradition tells us that Peter laid hold of his unity with Christ and when escaping for his life from Rome, he met Christ at the gate to the city, who, upon Peter's asking Him where He was going, Christ replied, "I have come to be crucified again." Peter, seeing his own life as bound up with Christ's, returned to the city and was crucified.

John the Beloved

The beloved John accepted the life of Christ and recognised the gift for every individual. He loved others as Christ first loved him. I would like here to insert a wonderful story of God's love toward the sinner.

> After the death of the tyrant, when John was returned to Ephesus, from the Isle of Patmos, he was desired to resort to the places bordering near unto him, partly to constitute bishops, partly to dispose the causes and matters of the church, partly to ordain and set such of the clergy in office whom the Holy Ghost should elect. Whereupon, when he was come to a certain city not far off, the name of which also many do yet remember, and had among other things comforted the brethren, he, looking more earnestly upon him which was the chief bishop among them, beheld a young man mighty in body, and of beautiful countenance, and of a fervent mind: "I commend this man," he said, "to thee with great diligence, in witness here of Christ and of the church."
>
> When the bishop had received of him this charge, and had promised his faithful diligence therein; again, the second time John spake unto him, and desired him in like manner and contestation as before. This done, John returned to Ephesus. The bishop, receiving the young man commended and committed to his charge, brought him home, kept him, and nourished him, and at length also did illuminate (that is, he baptized) him, and in short time through his diligence brought him into such order and towardness, that he committed unto him the oversight of a certain cure in the Lord's behalf.
>
> The young man having thus more his liberty, it chanced that

certain of his companions and old familiars being idle, dissolute, and accustomed of old time to wickedness, did join in company with him, who first brought him to sumptuous and riotous banquets; then incited him forth with them in the night to rob and steal; after that he was allured by them unto greater mischief and wickedness. Wherein by custom of time, by little and little, he being more practised, and being of good wit and a stout courage, like unto a wild or unbroken horse, leaving the right way, and running at large without bridle, was carried headlong to the profundity of all misorder and outrage. And thus, being past all hope of grace, utterly forgetting and rejecting the wholesome doctrine of salvation, which he had learned before, began to set his mind upon no small matters. And forasmuch as he was entered so far in the way of perdition, he cared not how much farther he proceeded in the same. And so, associating unto him the company of his companions and fellow thieves, took upon him to be as head and captain among them in committing and kinds of murder and felony.

In the meantime, it chanced that of necessity John was sent for to those quarters again, and came. The causes being decided, and his business ended for the which he came, by the way meeting with the bishop afore specified, he requireth of him the pledge, which in the witness of Christ and of the congregation then present he left in his hands to keep. The bishop, something amazed at the words of John, supposing he had meant of some money committed to his custody which he had not received, (and yet durst not mistrust John, nor contrary his words,) could not tell what to answer.

Then John perceiving his doubting, and uttering his mind more plainly, "The young man," he said, "and the soul of our brother committed to your custody, I do require."

Then the bishop with a loud voice sorrowing and weeping said, "He is dead."

To whom John said, "How, and by what death?"

The other said, "He is dead to God; for he is become an evil man and pernicious; to be brief, a thief; and now he doth frequent this mountain with a company of villains like unto himself against the church."

But the apostle rent his garments, and with great lamentation said, "I have left a good keeper of my brother's soul; get me a horse, and let me have a guide with me;" which being done, his horse and man procured, he hasted from the church as much as he could, and coming to the same place, was taken of thieves that watched. But he, neither flying nor refusing, said, "I came for this same cause thither; lead me," said he, "to your captain."

So he being brought, the captain, all armed, fiercely began to look upon him; and eftsoons coming to the knowledge of him, was stricken with confusion and shame, and began to fly. But the old man followed him as much as he might, forgetting his age, and crying, "My son, why dost thou fly from thy father? An armed man from one naked, a young man from an old man? Have pity on me, my son, and fear not, for there is yet hope of salvation; I will make answer for thee unto Christ; I will die for thee if need be; as Christ hath died for us, I will give my life for thee; believe me, Christ hath sent me."

He hearing these things, first as in a maze stood still, and therewith his courage was abated. After that he had cast down his weapons, by and by he trembled, yea, and wept bitterly; and coming to the old man, embraced him, and spake unto him with weeping, (as well as he could,) being even then baptized afresh with tears, only his right hand being hid and covered. Then the apostle, after that he had promised and firmly ascertained him that he should obtain remission from our Saviour, and also prayed, falling down upon his knees, and kissed his murdering right hand, which for shame he durst not show before, as now purged through repentance, brought him to the congregation. And when he had prayed for him with continual prayers and daily fastings, and had comforted and confirmed his mind with many sentences, went not from him before he had restored him to the congregation, and made him a great example and trial of regeneration, and a token of visible regeneration.

John Foxe, *Foxe's Book of Martyrs*, Volume 1, page 29.

The Apostle Paul

The Apostle Paul speaks that which everyone of us has the right to say:

"I am crucified with Christ: nevertheless I live; yet not I, but Christ liveth in me: and the life which I now live in the flesh I live by the faith of the Son of God, who loved me, and gave himself for me" (Galatians 2:20).

Summarizing this life in Christ, he says "For me to live is Christ" (Philippians 1:21).

Martin Luther

Martin Luther taught a personal Saviour. He declared:

> Faith must be purely taught namely, that thou art so entirely joined unto Christ, that He and thou art made as it were one person: so that thou mayest boldly say, I am now one with Christ, that is to say, Christ's righteousness, victory and life are mine. And again, Christ may say, I am that sinner, that is, his sins and his death are Mine, because he is united and joined unto Me, and I unto him. For by faith we are so joined together that we are become members of His body, of His flesh and of His bones (Ephesians 5:30).
>
> Martin Luther, *Commentary on Galatians*, Galatians 2:20.

And speaking further in his comments, Luther says that Christ:

> Took upon Him our sinful person, and gave unto us His innocent and victorious person; wherewith we being now clothed, are freed from the curse of the law. For Christ was willingly made a curse for us, saying, as touching My own person, I am blessed and need nothing. But I will abase Myself and will put upon Me your person... and will suffer death, to deliver you from death...
>
> This image and this mirror we must have continually before us, and behold the same with a steadfast eye of faith. He that doth so, hath this innocency and victory of Christ, although he be never so great a sinner. By faith only therefore we are made righteousness, for faith layeth hold of this innocency and victory of Christ. Look then how much thou believest this, so much dost thou enjoy it...
>
> ...If thou believe, sin, death and the curse to be abolished, they are abolished. For Christ hath overcome and taken away these in Himself, and will have us to believe that like as in His own person, there is no sin or death, even so there is none in ours, seeing He has performed and accomplished all things for us. Wherefore if sin vex thee and terrify thee, think that it is (as indeed it is) but an imagination, and a false illusion of the devil. For in very deed there is now no sin, no curse, no death, no devil, to hurt us any more, for Christ hath vanquished and abolished all

these things. The victory of Christ is most certain and there is no defect in the thing itself but in our incredulity (unbelief).

Ibid., Galatians 3:13.

This is an accurate revelation of how God really sees things – for the dead live unto Him and He counts "those things which be not as though they were" (Luke 20:28; Romans 4:17). Already Satan has been vanquished, the problem of sin has been solved, and we sit with Him in heavenly places. When our faith is perfect, this will be our reality.

John Bunyan

John Bunyan was a desperate man, and Christ did not fail to identify Himself to him. Writing in the autobiographical account of his conversion, Bunyan writes:

> The Lord did also lead me into the mystery of union with the Son of God; that I was joined to Him, that I was flesh of His flesh, and bone of His bone; ... for if He and I were one, then His righteousness was mine, His merits mine, His victory also mine. Now could I see myself in heaven and earth at once: in heaven by my Christ, by my head, by my righteousness and life, though on earth by my body or person.

John Bunyan, *Grace Abounding to the Chief of Sinners*.

Charles Spurgeon

Charles Spurgeon writes that:

> By divine decree, there existed such an union between Christ and his people, that all Christ did his people did: and all Christ has performed, his people did perform in him, for they were in his loins when he descended to the tomb, and in his loins they have ascended up on high; with him they entered into bliss; and with him they sit in heavenly places.

Charles Spurgeon, Sermon: *Christ in the Covenant*.

The desperate

Over the centuries, many have laid hold of this wonderful truth and been mocked and ridiculed and suffered on its behalf.

But no matter what the consequences may be, the truth of what God and Christ have really done for us must be told. Not a single fraction of the eternally abounding grace of God can be kept from the mind and hearts of those who are desperately seeking a solution to life's problems. This truth will encircle the earth with glory, and then the end shall come, for God will see His life perfectly reproduced in those who will to be saved, and He will come and take them home.

The charge of blasphemy against Christ will be hurled at His followers today

That God can become at one with us is not a myth. In Christ's day it was regarded as blasphemy that a man would claim to be God! And today, it is regarded as blasphemy to claim that God became man. But even worse, a particular man? Perhaps one we know personally? Even ourselves. Despite all reactions, I cry, "Give me such a Jesus, for nothing less will save me!"

If many religions in this world have the liberty to declare that every individual is Christ, then we claim the right to declare the truth – that Christ identified Himself so perfectly with the individual that He became "me". God is God. He can do whatever He wants, whatever He needs to do for our salvation. He can become "us" if He so desires and our salvation requires it. But we can never become Him. It only works one way. There is but one power that Satan has not taken from us and that is the power of choice. We can choose to let go and let God. And the amazing thing is that God will then count all of His right-doing within us, as our own. But we will ascribe all glory praise and honour unto God.

What greater declaration of God's love is there? Has it ever been said to you by others that they are glad that they are not you? Or that they are glad that they're not in your shoes? Well, Christ says, "I am you. I am not ashamed to be you. And let's work out life's problems together." He knows exactly where the shoe pinches because He is walking in the same shoes with you and feeling the pinch just as you are feeling it.

We do not become God

A few things must be kept plain. None of what God offers us is ours by right, or by title, but only by mercy and adoption. None is ours inherently, but by inheritance. This is made possible only by God becoming completely at one with us. It is nothing to do with us becoming God, but that God adopts us into His family. It is not humanity reaching out to the divinity, but divinity reaching out to humanity. It was divinity that took humanity into itself. Humanity did not take divinity into itself. We do not become divine. We do not evolve to a higher state of existence. Only God is self-existent. We are not. We can never exist as God. But it can work the other way because God is not limited.

Christ did not bring the attributes of divinity into our human nature; they are only ours as a gift when the human is united with the divinity of God. Even though we are one with Him, His attributes will never be inherent in humanity of itself. What Christ did was return human nature to what it once was according to God's original plan. In heaven, we will share His throne, but we will not share in His right to be worshipped – we will worship Him. We will reign with Him, but only as beside Him upon the throne. We will be priests, but He is the High Priest. We will officiate. But He is the official.

A life that measures with the life of God

And herein is the gift of Jesus. A life that can be ours today if we will only accept it. Are you desperate enough for it? Or are you waiting for your life to fall down around you before you recognize your utter need? Tarry not. There is not much time left to lay hold of this gift.

But why delay? If the life that Christ lived was my own life, and it was the Father that lived His own life in Him, then doesn't that mean that what God is offering us is a life that measures with the life of God? Of course! Because it is His life. And it is ours now, and forever after. Sounds pretty good to me!

A prayer

"I thank you God that you have not left me to try and work things out myself. I am sorry that so many times I have pushed you away and taken things into my own hands. You have graciously stepped back and waited patiently for me to realise that I cannot do anything right without you. You gave me my life but I haven't taken very good care of it. And now I am afraid to live my own life because I know I'll only mess things up. Please, will you live it for me now? I humbly ask you that you will give me the same perfect life that you have lived in Jesus because I believe that it is my own life, prepared especially for me. If I should snatch my life back and wreck it again, please don't let me harden my heart and try and fix it myself. Send your Holy Spirit to awaken me once more to my desperate need. And help me to fall, finally, once and for all, completely broken at the feet of your dear Son and never again to take my own life into my own hands. Only you can I trust. Only you do I trust. And I thank you for what you have promised to do for I believe that you will do all things well just as long as I let you do all things. I ask these things in the name of your dear Son, Jesus Christ. Amen."

www.ingramcontent.com/pod-product-compliance
Lightning Source LLC
Chambersburg PA
CBHW051958290426
44110CB00015B/2298